MW01065069

CAREER EXPLORATION

Computer Programmer

by Rosemary Wallner

Consultant:
Virginia T. Anderson, Ph.D.
Lecturer, Computer Science (Ret.)
University of North Dakota

CAPSTONE BOOKS

an imprint of Capstone Press
Mankato, Minnesota

Capstone Books are published by Capstone Press
151 Good Counsel Drive, P.O. Box 669, Mankato, Minnesota 56002
http://www.capstone-press.com

Library of Congress Cataloging-in-Publication Data
Wallner, Rosemary, 1964–
    Computer programmer/by Rosemary Wallner.
    p. cm.—(Career exploration)
    Includes bibliographical references and index.
    Summary: An introduction to the career of computer programmer, including
discussion of educational requirements, duties, workplace, salary, employment
outlook, and possible future positions.
    ISBN 0-7368-0488-9
    1. Computer programming—Vocational guidance—Juvenile literature.
[1. Programming (Computers)—Vocational guidance. 2. Vocational guidance.]
I. Title. II. Series.
QA76.25 .W35 2000
005.3'023'73—dc21   99-052836

Editorial Credits

Leah K. Pockrandt, editor; Steve Christensen, cover designer; Kia Bielke, production
    designer and illustrator; Heidi Schoof, photo researcher

Photo Credits

David F. Clobes, cover, 8, 12
Diane Meyer, 35
Gregg R. Andersen, 6, 11, 14, 17, 18, 22, 25, 28, 36, 46
Hewlett-Packard Company, 21, 38
Photo Network/bachmann, 31
Shaffer Photography/James L. Shaffer, 33
Uniphoto/Charles Gupton, 41

1 2 3 4 5 6 05 04 03 02 01 00

Table of Contents

Fast Facts

Career Title	Computer Programmer
O*NET Number	25105
DOT Cluster (Dictionary of Occupational Titles)	Professional, technical, and managerial occupations
DOT Number	030.162-010
GOE Number (Guide for Occupational Exploration)	11.01.01
NOC Number (National Occupational Classification-Canada)	2163
Salary Range (U.S. Bureau of Labor Statistics and Human Resources Development Canada, late 1990s figures)	U.S.: $22,700 to $65,200 Canada: $22,400 to $53,800 (Canadian dollars)
Minimum Educational Requirements	U.S.: bachelor's degree Canada: bachelor's degree
Certification/Licensing Requirements	U.S.: none Canada: none

Subject Knowledge	Administration and management; clerical; personnel and human resources; computers and electronics; design; mathematics; education and training; English; communications and media
Personal Abilities/Skills	Use logic and scientific thinking to solve a variety of complex problems; understand and use advanced math and statistics; make decisions and deal with problems; use computer technology to solve problems or process large amounts of information; speak and write clearly and accurately; use technical terms; use math and computer symbols; use complex charts and graphs
Job Outlook	U.S.: faster than average growth Canada: good
Personal Interests	Leading-Influencing: Interest in leading and influencing others through activities involving high-level verbal or numerical abilities
Similar Types of Jobs	Computer scientist; computer engineer; systems analyst; statistician; mathematician

Chapter 1

Computer Programmer

Computer programmers write, test, and maintain computer programs. Computer programs are detailed instructions that computers follow in order to perform certain tasks. Programs also are called software. Computer programmers make sure software correctly tells computers what to do. Programmers also are called software engineers.

Career Definition

Computers help people perform different tasks. People use computers for word processing. They write and store documents on computers. They also use computers to send e-mail messages and access the Internet. Some companies use computers to keep records of shipping and sales information.

Computer programmers write, test, and maintain a variety of computer programs.

Some companies use computers to operate large factory machines.

Other companies depend on computers to operate large machines such as factory equipment.

Computer programmers write software. They use computer keyboards to type sets of instructions for computers. These instructions are called source codes. Source codes consist of key word commands and mathematical equations.

Computer programmers use programming languages that computers can process. These include C, Visual Basic, and Java. Computer programmers usually know more than one programming language. Programmers can learn new computer languages easily because many languages are similar. Programmers' job titles often refer to the languages with which they work. Programmers' titles also can refer to the types of programs they write.

Computer programs are converted to electronic forms that computers can understand. This is done through compiler programs. The converted instructions are the program files. These converted programs actually do the work in computers. These programs are sold to customers as software.

Computer programmers must test and debug programs. Errors in programs are called bugs. Computer programmers debug programs by testing them. They try to find which parts of the source codes are causing errors.

Most computer programmers begin their careers as junior programmers. They receive direction from supervisors. Junior programmers may work alone on simple assignments. Many work as part of teams with more experienced programmers. Junior programmers usually do not have the experience to create complex programs.

How Computer Programs Work

Programs give computers instructions. Programs direct computers to gather and process different types of data. For example, one program may tell a computer how to direct large machines to assemble parts of a truck. Another program may tell a computer how to watch for changing weather conditions.

Computer programs include commands. Programs use a step-by-step process of small decisions that lead to a certain goal.

Computer programmers often use flowcharts to show program commands. Flowcharts represent the basic flow of information and ideas through a program. In a flowchart, boxes of different shapes represent different operations within a program. Lines connect the boxes. These lines represent the order of the command steps.

Where Programmers Work

Computer programmers work in a variety of settings. Most computer programmers work for data processing services or computer companies. Many of these companies write and sell computer programs. Some computer programmers work for companies that make computers, office equipment, or other products.

Some computer programmers telecommute. These programmers work at home for a company. They do not work in an office building. These

Programmers who telecommute may work in their company's office on certain days of the week.

programmers may use equipment such as modems and fax machines to communicate with their company. Modems are electronic devices that connect programmers' home computers to their company's computers. Programmers who telecommute may work in the company's office on certain days of the week. They also may attend company meetings.

Some programmers become specialists in such areas as networking, screen designing, or web page designing. These programmers work for companies that employ programmers with different specialties.

Many computer programmers are either applications or systems programmers.

These companies then supply specialized computer programmers to clients. Clients are people or businesses who need programs written for them. Clients may include manufacturing companies, schools, or banks. The companies match the needs of the clients to the programmers' specialties.

Some computer programmers are independent consultants or freelancers. These programmers do not work full-time for one company. They work for a company on a temporary or contract basis. People or companies hire these programmers to complete specific jobs. These programmers work only as long as they are needed to complete a job. Independent consultants often can set their own work hours and pay rates.

Specialty Areas

Computer programmers work in two areas. They either are applications or systems programmers.

Applications programmers write computer programs for specific tasks. They write programs for tasks such as word processing, accounting, or inventory control. They also may write programs for computer games.

Applications programmers often specialize in a certain field. This is called a subspecialty. They may specialize in business, science, or engineering.

Systems programmers maintain the software that controls entire operating computer systems. This system includes an operating computer that is connected to several other computers. An operating computer usually instructs all the other computers in the system. This system also may be called a mainframe. Systems programmers change the sets of instructions that tell the operating computer what to do. They make sure the mainframe is able to work with the computers and other equipment in the system.

Chapter 2

Day-to-Day Activities

Applications and systems programmers perform different tasks. But both types of programmers spend many hours working on programs. They create, update, and test programs.

Applications Programmers

Applications programmers start each project by meeting with a team of people. The team includes computer designers, artists, and other computer specialists. Computer designers tell programmers what the finished program should do. Computer artists show sketches of how the program should look on the computer screen. Other computer specialists tell how fast the program should work and who the program's users will be.

Applications programmers often spend many hours working on a program.

Applications programmers map out a strategy for the program. They make a flowchart to show the sequence of steps. They must know how fast the computers that will use the program operate. They also must know how much memory these computers have to store data. Applications programmers find the most difficult features of new programs. They work out ways to avoid trouble spots.

Applications programmers present different program ideas to their teams and clients. The programmers then write the program codes after their teams and clients approve the ideas.

Programmers also review, update, and modify programs. They modify programs by changing them to make the programs work faster or easier. The programmers meet with clients or program users to learn what changes must be made.

Systems Programmers

Systems programmers write and test specialized computer software called operating systems software. This type of software allows computers to use applications programs.

Systems programmers receive detailed instructions from supervisors or clients before they begin projects. These instructions may be about a

Applications programmers write the software after meeting with their teams and clients.

piece of computer hardware. Computer hardware includes internal parts of computers such as hard drives and disk drives. It also includes external parts such as printers, monitors, and keyboards. Systems programmers may need to write code to make two pieces of hardware work together. Later, the programmers may need to write code to make the central processing unit (CPU) work faster. This part of the computer processes all the commands.

Applications programmers sometimes meet with systems programmers. The programmers may

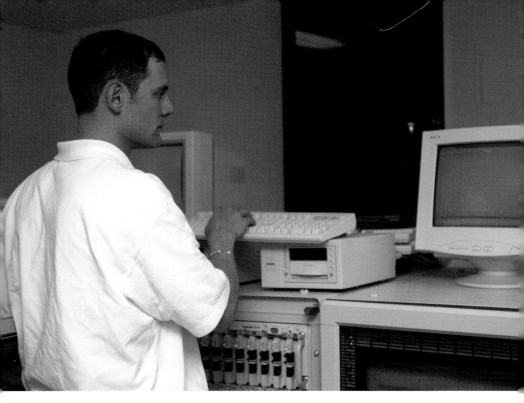

Some computer programmers work with a company's network or server.

discuss errors or trouble spots in programs. Systems and applications programmers may talk about the best ways to write and modify programs.

Systems programmers often help applications programmers. Systems programmers know about entire computer systems. They often can help applications programmers find and solve program problems.

Other Programmers

Some applications or systems programmers work on networks. Networks connect a company's computers to a central computer system. Employees can access information and store data on the central system. Such a system also allows employees to access the Internet and send or receive e-mail messages. Networks also may be called servers.

Some applications or systems programmers work on Internet programs. They may create the web sites or program the sites to perform functions or tasks.

Systems or applications programmers also may work as graphics programmers. These programmers design monitor screens. These include screen savers or desktop images.

Testing and Debugging Programs

Both applications and systems programmers must test their programs. They make sure the programs operate properly. Programmers test programs by running them. For example, a program may instruct a machine to attach a steering wheel inside a car. The computer programmer makes sure the program correctly instructs the computer to complete this task.

Applications and systems programmers must fix programs that have errors in them. Programmers must change and recheck the programs until they produce the correct results. Small errors in a source code can cause a program to run improperly. An error could be as simple as an extra comma or space.

Working with Others

Computer programmers often work in teams. A senior programmer usually oversees the programmers on a team. Many computer programmers may be needed to write programs that use complex math formulas. Programmers can work for more than a year to write, compile, test, and debug a program. On a team, each programmer writes one part of the program. The programmers then combine all the parts to make one program.

Some computer programmers must work closely with co-workers. These programmers must follow descriptions prepared by systems analysts or software engineers. Software engineers design the overall look of a program. Systems analysts connect workstation

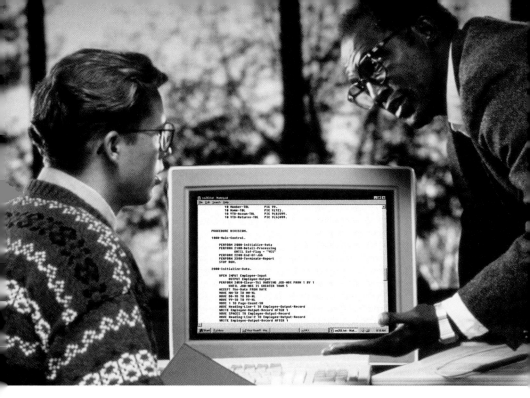

A senior programmer oversees the work of other computer programmers.

computers to the mainframe so that they can communicate. The descriptions provided by software engineers and systems analysts list several steps. A computer must follow these steps to process data and achieve the desired results.

Some computer programmers train co-workers. Programmers who know a great deal about certain programs may teach other employees how to use them.

Chapter 3

The Right Candidate

Computer programmers need a variety of skills and abilities. They must carefully think through problems and create solutions. They must be able to work well alone and with others.

Basic Skills

Computer programmers need technical knowledge. They must know and understand advanced math such as statistics. Programmers use their technical knowledge to solve problems and process large amounts of data. Programmers use technical terms, math, and computer symbols to create flowcharts and source codes.

Computer programmers must be able to analyze mathematical data. They work carefully

Computer programmers use their technical knowledge to create flowcharts.

with data in order to understand it. They use this understanding to write effective programs.

Abilities

Computer programmers must have good communication skills. They must be able to explain their ideas and opinions clearly. They must listen to other people's points of view. They also should be able to clearly express their ideas in writing.

Programmers also must communicate well with clients. They need to understand exactly what clients want programs to do. But sometimes clients do not know exactly what they want. This makes it difficult for programmers to complete their tasks. They then must ask detailed questions to understand their clients' needs.

Computer programmers must be able to work with people who do not understand computer technology. Programmers should be able to write a program that users can operate easily. Programmers may need to teach users how to operate programs.

Computer programmers use their knowledge and logic to solve complex problems.

Programmers need good problem-solving skills. They must know how to write programs to perform specific functions. Programmers must be able to troubleshoot or debug programs. They must use logic to solve many complex problems. Logic is clear and concise thinking. They also must use their imaginations to create solutions for program problems.

Skills

Workplace Skills   Yes / No

Resources:
Assign use of time .... ☑ ☐
Assign use of money .... ☐ ☑
Assign use of material and facility resources .... ☑ ☐
Assign use of human resources .... ☑ ☐

Interpersonal Skills:
Take part as a member of a team .... ☑ ☐
Teach others .... ☑ ☐
Serve clients/customers .... ☑ ☐
Show leadership .... ☑ ☐
Work with others to arrive at a decision .... ☑ ☐
Work with a variety of people .... ☑ ☐

Information:
Acquire and judge information .... ☑ ☐
Understand and follow legal requirements .... ☑ ☐
Organize and maintain information .... ☑ ☐
Understand and communicate information .... ☑ ☐
Use computers to process information .... ☑ ☐

Systems:
Identify, understand, and work with systems .... ☑ ☐
Understand environmental, social, political, economic,
    or business systems .... ☑ ☐
Oversee and correct system performance .... ☑ ☐
Improve and create systems .... ☑ ☐

Technology:
Select technology .... ☑ ☐
Apply technology to task .... ☑ ☐
Maintain and troubleshoot technology .... ☑ ☐

Foundation Skills

Basic Skills:
Read .... ☑ ☐
Write .... ☑ ☐
Do arithmetic and math .... ☑ ☐
Speak and listen .... ☑ ☐

Thinking Skills:
Learn .... ☑ ☐
Reason .... ☑ ☐
Think creatively .... ☑ ☐
Make decisions .... ☑ ☐
Solve problems .... ☑ ☐

Personal Qualities:
Take individual responsibility .... ☑ ☐
Have self-esteem and self-management .... ☑ ☐
Be sociable .... ☑ ☐
Be fair, honest, and sincere .... ☑ ☐

Computer programmers use logic to write programs. Programmers use a step-by-step process of small decisions to achieve their goals. Computer programmers must know every task computers must perform. They also must know the order in which computers will do these tasks.

Work Styles

Computer programmers must be patient and persistent. They must continue to work on a program and not give up. They must be able to remain calm despite problems.

Programmers must manage their time well. They need to meet deadlines. These times are when projects must be finished. Computer programmers need to complete their work even while under pressure from supervisors or clients.

Chapter 4

Preparing for the Career

Computer programmers need to know a great deal about computers and how they work. They usually learn this technical information at colleges or universities.

High School Education

High school students who want to become computer programmers should take computer courses. Some schools offer classes in keyboarding, basic computer skills, or simple programming.

High school students also should take courses in math, science, English, and speech. Students learn how to use logic and step-by-step problem solving in math classes. They learn how to study technical

Computer programmers attend colleges or universities to learn about computers and how they work.

information in science classes. Students learn how to write in English classes. They learn how to share their ideas and communicate in speech classes.

High school students may benefit from working on computers outside of school. Many students have a computer at home. They can study computer program manuals or use their computers to practice writing programs. Students may use the Internet or e-mail. Many libraries also have computers that students can use. Students also may join computer science clubs to learn more about computers.

Students may work at stores that sell computers. They can learn about different programs and equipment through this experience. They also will learn how to work with other people such as fellow employees and customers.

Post-Secondary Education

Computer programmers need a bachelor's degree. It usually takes students about four years to earn a bachelor's degree from a college or university. Students should earn their degree in computer science or another computer-related field.

Computer programming students learn computer languages. Students learn the most popular languages first. These include FORTRAN, COBOL, and C. Other important languages

High school students gain knowledge about computers by working on them.

include CASE tools, C++, Ada, Smalltalk, Visual Basic, PowerBuilder, and Java.

Students also study computer operating systems. They take courses in computer programming. They learn about different types of hardware. They learn how to write code so that different pieces of hardware can work together.

Students also may benefit from taking courses or earning a degree in other fields. These fields include business, accounting, and engineering.

Students study management and inventory control in business classes. They study ways to keep financial records in accounting classes. Students study how machines work in engineering and physics classes. This knowledge can help computer programmers write software for those fields.

Internship Programs
Most employers prefer to hire graduates with previous computer experience. They want programmers who have technical experience. They also want programmers who can adapt to new situations and learn new skills.

College students can gain experience through internship programs. Students work with computer professionals in internship programs. Student interns learn about the profession from these programmers. Many colleges offer internships with computer companies. Students perform internships during the summer or during an extra semester or year of college. Some interns are paid for their work.

Certification
Computer programmers do not need certification or licensing to perform their jobs. But some employers may encourage their employees to earn

Business classes may help programmers write software for different companies.

certification in a certain area. Certification means that a person is qualified to perform a job. Computer programming organizations and computer product manufacturers offer certification programs to computer programmers.

The Institute for Certification of Computing Professionals (ICCP) is an organization that offers certification for computer programmers. Programmers who have a bachelor's degree and two years of experience may earn the title Certified

Computing Professional (CCP). Programmers without a degree also may earn this title. These programmers must have at least four years of programming experience. Programmers must pass a general exam and two specialty area exams to qualify for this certificate.

Programmers with little or no experience also may become certified. They may be certified as an Associate Computer Professional (ACP). They must pass a test to earn this certificate.

Continuing Education

Some computer programmers may want to continue their education. They may earn a master's degree in a computer-related field such as computer engineering. They earn this degree by completing advanced courses and research in a certain subject. Students usually earn a master's degree in about three years. Some students may earn a doctoral degree. This is the highest degree offered by some universities. Doctoral degrees require advanced study and may take several years to complete.

Computer programmers must continue to learn as technology changes.

Computer programmers must keep up with new computer developments and information. Computer technology changes rapidly. Computer programmers can learn about new programming methods or equipment at professional seminars and workshops. They can listen to and talk with other professionals at these activities. Computer programmers also can learn new information by reading professional journals and other publications.

Chapter 5

The Market

The job market is strong for computer programmers. Businesses need systems and applications programmers to stay current with changing technology. Computer programmers' job opportunities and salaries are based on their experience and education. Programmers who keep up with programming languages and techniques will be the most successful.

Salary

In the United States, computer programmers earn between $22,700 and $65,200 per year. The average annual salary for computer programmers is about $40,000. Salaries also are based on job location. Most software companies are located in the West and Northeast. Computer programmers in these areas earn more than

Computer programmers' job opportunities are based on experience.

Some computer programmers open their own computer consulting businesses.

programmers in the South and Midwest. Systems programmers also earn more than applications programmers.

In Canada, computer programmers earn between $22,400 and $53,800 per year. The average annual salary for computer programmers in Canada is $38,100.

Job Outlook

In the United States, the job outlook for computer programmers is expected to have faster than average growth. Many jobs will be available for systems and applications programmers in data processing service firms. Software companies and computer consulting businesses also will have many job openings. Companies will need programmers to help improve or convert their computer programs and systems.

In Canada, the job outlook for computer programmers is good. But the labor market for programmers is weaker than the market for more advanced computer analysts. Computer analysts often are responsible for designing an entire computer system or product.

Advancement Opportunities

Computer programmers may advance depending on their experience. Junior programmers may advance to become senior programmers. These programmers work independently within teams. They earn higher salaries than junior programmers do. But they work more hours than junior programmers do. Senior programmers code and debug programs written by junior programmers. They may meet with company executives and clients. Senior programmers may travel to a client's company to discuss the client's programming needs.

Senior programmers may advance in several ways. Some senior programmers start their own computer consulting businesses. Some programmers advance to jobs as systems analysts or managers. Management positions may include becoming a project or team leader. Project leaders oversee a team of programmers and manage operating systems.

Related Careers

People interested in computers, math, and other technical fields have many career opportunities. Careers that have similar interest areas include computer analysts, computer product design engineers, or accountants. Computer product design engineers work with computer designers to develop new computer hardware. An accountant is an expert on money matters.

People interested in computers, math, or other technical fields may become engineers.

The need for programmers will continue to increase as technology advances. More products and services rely on computers to operate. Programmers will be needed to write programs that produce or control such items. Businesses also need programmers to provide software to aid in their day-to-day operations.

Words to Know

data (DAY-tuh)—information or facts

debug (dee-BUHG)— to find which parts of a code are causing errors and then rewrite the code to remove the errors

hardware (HARD-wair)—computer equipment; hardware includes internal parts of a computer as well as printers, monitors, or keyboards.

modem (MOH-duhm)—a piece of electronic equipment used to send information between computers by telephone lines

program (PROH-gram)—a series of instructions written in a computer language; programs control the way a computer works.

software (SAWFT-wair)—computer programs that control the workings of the equipment or hardware and direct it to do specific tasks

technology (tek-NOL-uh-jee)—the use of science and engineering to do practical things such as build machines or other products

telecommute (tel-uh-kuh-MYOOT)—to work at home or at a remote location; telecommuters often use a computer with modem, a fax machine, or other form of electronic communication.

troubleshoot (TRUH-buhl-shoot)—to work on a problem until a solution is found; to find the cause of a problem.

To Learn More

Burns, Julie Kling. *Opportunities in Computer Systems Careers: Software.* VGM Opportunities. Lincolnwood, Ill.: VGM Career Horizons, 1996.

Cosgrove, Holli, ed. *Career Discovery Encyclopedia.* Vol. 2. Chicago: Ferguson Publishing, 2000.

Henderson, Harry. *Career Opportunities in Computers and Cyberspace.* New York: Facts on File, 1999.

Reeves, Diane Lindsey, and Peter Kent. *Career Ideas for Kids Who Like Computers.* New York: Facts on File, 1998.

Useful Addresses

**Canadian Society for Computational Studies
of Intelligence (CSCSI)**
CIPS National Office
One Yonge Street
Suite 2401
Toronto, ON M5E 1E5
Canada

IEEE Computer Society
Headquarters Office
1730 Massachusetts Avenue NW
Washington, DC 20036

**Institute for Certification of Computing
Professionals**
2200 East Devon Avenue
Suite 247
Des Plaines, IL 60018

Internet Sites

American Electronics Association
http://www.aeanet.org

Association of Information Technology Professionals (AITP)
http://www.aitp.org

Institute for Certification of Computing Professionals (ICCP)
http://www.iccp.org

Job Futures—Computer Programmers
http://www.hrdc-drhc.gc.ca/JobFutures/english/volume1/2163/2163.htm

Occupational Outlook Handbook— Computer Programmers
http://stats.bls.gov/oco/ocos110.htm

Index